THE TRUTH LIES ON EARTH:

A YEAR BY DARK, BY BRIGHT

THE TRUTH LIES ON EARTH:

A Year by Dark, by Bright

By Peter Neil Carroll

First Edition

Published by Turning Point Books
P.O. Box 541106
Cincinnati, OH 45254-1106
www.turningpointbooks.com

Manufactured in the USA.

Cover photograph: *TBD*, Jeannette Ferrary, ©2016

Designed by Debra Turner

ISBN: 9781625492180

To the Memory of My Parents
Louis S. Carroll
Bessie Nurko Carroll

"Everything the Power of the World does is done in a circle...
Even the seasons form a great circle in their changing."
— *Black Elk Speaks*

"They call this Spring, Mum, and they have one every year."
— Letter from an English child evacuated
to the countryside for safety, 1940.

Contents

PART 3   "to study the light"

PART 4   "before the real drama begins"

PART 5   "no matter how lonely"

PART I

time to start over

The First of Winter

The ocean roars in darkness, pounding
black rock until that throbbing heartbeat
breaches the bulwarks of my body, muscles
synchronized, the way gravity forces
two pendulums to align. Even at midnight,
white spume captures starlight, illuminating
a room at the edge of Earth. Next to me
she begins to breathe audibly, enters
a rhythm identical to mine and the ocean's.
Outside, nothing visible is alive—no plant,
bird, creature of the sea. Nothing is dead.

At dawn, a solitary gull skates inches
above the rolling crests, skimming
rock cod, snapper, crab. A dog stands
in white froth mesmerized by what eludes
his snout and runs out. Daylight belongs
to shivering fishers on the pier—men,
old women speaking dialects—the sun
softening the ocean's blow, their fear.

The smell of salt invigorates action,
men chopping raw chickens, packing
flesh into cages, tossed to the waves
as bait. In a minute, up comes the net
picked clean, causing marvel and mirth,
only then they glimpse the sleek culprit
silent as a cat burglar, fat seal diving down
their lines, surfacing, a whiskery smirk.

By noon, surfers triumph, flaunt the same
persistence as the waves they attempt
to subdue, as if patience has its reward.
Uncurious about depths or the falling sun,
back to land, ever in-bound, aimless
but for wind and tide, they dunk, they rise,
the perfect wave denies the endless ride.

Dusk, a rose flowers in the western sky, paints
gaps between broken shale, isles uninhabited
but for waterborne mammals, cormorants,
shipwrecks. Light fades, we slurp oysters pulled
from saline sleep, count rows of breaking waves—
never more than three lines at once—as one
in three ascends the steamy glass. Endlessly,
global, planetary. If there's an eternity,
we found it. If not, here's a good place to wait.

Hoppin' John

Fog hangs all night like cotton-wool
on drowsy willows, the new year
slowly wakening. A pigeon stalks
along the sill, looks me in the eye.

Back I stare, amazed at time's toll,
that far January First, chance unlocking
choice. Young that winter, I shovel snow,
she invites me in for a cup of mercy.

She warms me in her steamy kitchen,
black-eyed peas soaking all day, boiled
with onion, rice, vinegar-drenched greens.
Hoppin' John, she says, foreseeing luck.

That irreversible moment: jumping over
the broomstick, a lark, a sacred promise—
but a tie that age unbinds, separating us
from those we miss, its kiss irresistible.

Pea-jon, I breathe, pondering my visitor.
First day we meet again, time to start over.

Turning

I was a coffee man, straight shots in the morning,
eyes wide like this fellow with slender hips who steps
from the yellow taxi, turning
to help his girlfriend out, reaching
through the window to pay the driver.
She's about to enter the café, when he turns
her around, holds his phone near her face, captures
the nervous smile
framed by doorway and menu board.
He is black-skinned, she pallid and blonde
and hard to tell if it's the end
of a one-night stand or the second week.
Either way, she knows to follow instructions
as he turns her again, presses her
to an inside table, only a pane of glass
separating their intimacy from my solitude
outside. He orders for them both.
Me, I learned by loss, first ask.

Dogpatch, San Francisco

I wander sidewalks, a bowl of soup
on my mind, maybe chili or tuna
on toast, peek through the glass
at Hard Knox. Two women, 40s,
early 50s, just being served pie
and coffee, I take a stool at the bar,
hear the click of forks on plates,
their voices intimate, clear.

I put the stories together by pieces,
the one woman followed her lover
from somewhere like Peru or Chile
and after the army captured her town
had no choice but to stay. Her guy
loved cakes she made with spices
her sisters sent from home, they had
daughters. He died in a plane crash.

The other came alone from Italy
to study languages, stayed to teach
her native tongue. She found no men
worth a week's trouble, by herself
dealt with breast cancer, unaware
her hair had whitened at the edges.
They mention "Charles," discuss why
it took him so long to settle down,
a topic they stuck on without answer.

For an hour they prattle, pretending
I'm not here. Maybe I got the facts
wrong. But as they add the check
and stand up, giving each other a hug,
one turns, thanks me for listening.

The Nearness of Her

Soundless dawn, but for the nearness
of my favorite woodpecker, drilling
her beak into a sleepy oak. Forty years
I've lived on this street, seldom hear
a peep from the other neighbors.

Nat and Patty split up, he disappeared.
Dave, Ralph, Dale—the men drop
like overripe fruit. Their kids mature,
move away, slouch back. Widows stay,
indoors. I wonder what they do.

Maybe being so close explains tall
fences, shuttered gates. Maybe shame
of seeming too lonely. Maybe a fear
of falling for an old fool. Maybe
they already have my cup of sugar.

Digging In

I've dug in deeper, invited my trees
to circle the land, forming a windbreak,
a veil. Safer to live in shadow,
no saviors come to ring my bells.

After the ravens invaded, blue jays
vanished but this morning one returned
yapping, drunk on the red berries
of the firethorn bush.

The axis tilts but my neighbors stay.
Mrs. McCoy moved in when she was 30,
celebrates her 90TH year. In eight houses,
five men died. Their cars sit in rust.

I might try to know them better
but living close incites privacy.
Only the sound of motors, stray voices,
tell who's where. No more.

The Neighbors

I see Fireman Fred in a dream, picture
of health, he doesn't mention the wall
of smoke that put him underground
but shows the hot tub behind his house,
a telescope to navigate the night. He
says, *the stars are really gleaming,*
makes me feel I hadn't done enough,
but I know he's only the stand-in
for Walter next door stuck in his bed.

Downhill, Walter warms his bones
in afternoon sun, skin orange
as his batteries run down, winter
his last touch of Earth out-of-doors.
Fog approaches, its gray wool chilling,
his wife guides the blanketed man inside,
their arms linked. Her hand cups
the back of his drooped head.
He'll never cross the path separating
his house from mine. I walk toward them
at the front steps. His eyes shine. I ask
about the children. He gasps, lips stiff.
She explains that Walter has too much
to say, says she's making soup for lunch,
that's easy to eat—and I rush to my errands
as Walter meets the uncluttered day.

Patty keeps to herself, doesn't know
how much we know. Two seasons
since she told us Walter was sick.
She smiles through the car window.
We won't trespass to ask. They hold
the truth, as if cancer's contagious.

✳

A gift for my ailing neighbor— red chard,
white beans, onion, carrots simmering
in stock. Steam rises from the spoon.
I knock at his door but he's gone
already. Two days. Why didn't I know
grief travels so slowly between homes?

Survival Kit

My backyard shack, warehouse of mildewed magazines,
antique tax receipts, a dot-matrix printer—I come here
to clarify what's left and why a shelf of TV scripts
from the 70's still makes me laugh, the old actor ranting
at his children as I speak fears for my own kids,
grown and gone.

Behind spider webs waits my son's SURVIVAL KIT—
inside, a well-rubbed deck of cards for solitaire,
brittle sticks of gum, dried out licorice, a jar filled
with peanut shells. He was the hungriest boy.

His crayon-illustrated Joke Book begins
"What goes ha-ha-ha thump?"
Answer on the next page,
"A man laughing his head off."

I lift his deflated football, my stiff fingers bend
to the leather, wrist rises, elbows spread, he cuts
across the grass, the ball sails. . . .and under
the ball a silver needle to inflate the bladder.

We had a pact with Fireman Fred and his son:
they'd keep the air pump, we'd watch the pin.

I hold the relic between thumb and forefinger
not quite a Greek trophy but a voucher
from mornings we played at heroes.

I place it where I found it, as if offering a gift
to the gods could bring back anything we had.

Before Sunrise

Across the bed her head hidden
under pillows,
ears padded with cotton,
she pretends
not very well
not to be disturbed
all night
by an old man's exhaust.

The still willow in front
of the dark house
holds the morning odor
close to its armpits. A breeze
does not speak. The owl
who wooed me awake
has since fallen in love
with silence.

No feint of dawn, no need
for anyone's permission
to pause naked at the window,
to sight creamy stars pulsing
through sleepy leaves,
the entire world at rest
waits for that moment
before the lights go on.

In the Fourth Year of Drought

Soft as firewood ash, the sky wakens,
a weary willow leans toward dust.
Pines are vacant, ravens notorious
for morning rackets have sailed west
to the coast. They know where to go.

In the garden yellowing stalks predict
rising prices of lettuce. For months
I've gathered gray water to satiate
the olive tree that makes no promises.
Dishes sit in the sink. I crave ice cubes.

I'm reminded of the Dust Bowl widow
who abandoned wilted corn in Nebraska
to pick fruit in California, lamenting
she no longer had a mailbox address, no
one could find her. But I'm not leaving.

Just yesterday, I skipped my shower, went
for a walk, returned to find someone had
left a jar of sun tea brewing in the yard. Now
I smell fog coming in to shroud my thirst
with hope, low clouds cozier than fire.

PART 2

to seed our little clump

White Fields Waiting

Two weeks before spring equinox, wisps
of pollen powder the yard. Any minute
the fog will lift, inviting hummingbirds
to jitterbug with my budding magnolia.

Back east, it's snowing. As my fire leaps
into dry sky, ten inches have fallen there,
exciting memories of swollen cloud,
wind stuttering first flurries. At dawn,

the milk truck would pioneer a trail.
In boots buckled with metal latches
I attacked virgin yards, bashed snowballs
against trees and slow-moving cars.

I picture white fields waiting for a boy.
My mother also waits, though I'm going
gray. Outside bees are singing to lemon
sugar, sirens begging me not to go home.

Anonymity

The old man in me returns alone
to walk grizzled blocks, passes
the Armory's brass plaque
marking the 1915 art show
that names no artist, only
fat cats who put up the sign.

Fortress doors locked,
I hike over to Madison park,
too cold for mothers pushing
carriages, and wander east
to admire those sturdy taverns
on Lexington near 23rd.

The wind picks up, flurries
zig-zagging the sky, I bury
my chin in a soft muffler.
Kitty-corner at the curb
a steaming food cart waits,
bathes me in blue fumes.

Stone walls stand as they stood,
as painters in the Armory show
live amid anonymity. Loneliness
is a way of life. The city doesn't
grieve, though my eyes are tearing,
my mouth eager for burnt chestnuts.

Amherst

Outside the Dickinson house, cold bites
zero deep as I amble white streets.
I pass bright-painted houses where black
servants brought from Dixie
discovered snow and stayed to raise free
children. An orchard of apple trees
shades the separate gardens. Frozen
air dampens sound. A collie at the edge
of a porch declines to speak, his quiet
shimmering my inner light.

Destiny

She did not know what she was thinking
during the dark hours she waited
until her husband began to snore.
That gave her permission. Slipping
from bed, she grabbed her hooded coat,
fur-lined boots, unlocked the storm door
to face the icy stars.

She had no intention, swaying
on the rope swing, hoping
a comet would burn up the sky.
When that didn't happen
she took it as an omen
anyway, certain she would perish
in the cold Midwestern night
if she didn't leave for California.

That's the first story she told me.
At last I knew where I'd wind up.

Winter Light

Inside the fast car, sun glares
between snow-bound trees, forces
an involuntary wink, opens
a long-shut memory.

My dad's brother, watching
Friday night fights, shadow-boxed
into a heart attack, dead
said his wife, before he hit the rug.

Fear I felt, of what I might need
to see—a face, his fate.
He looks, someone said,
like he'll sit up in a minute.

I saw my father cry
for the first time.
No one offered me sympathy.
No one had to.

Dry-eyed, I knew exactly where
I was bound by blood, a rider
in the back seat. I kept
my eyes on the mottled sky.

Steam Heat

Even in winter I like open
windows, radiators shut,
a preference my widowed aunt
discovered the first night
she arrived, slept in my room.

She came down in the morning
not to complain, but bragged
how she'd used her strong arms,
figured out how to turn the valves
that brought in steam heat.

What she required she'd find
in herself, unique in my family,
women counting on men. I saw
the kind of woman I wanted:
someone who'd rather take care
alone than bang on my pipes.

Sparrows

Outside the chilly panes
only sparrows fly, feathers
smudged as city snow. Grandma
liked to leave stale bread
on the fire escape, but me
she gave chocolate cherries,
teasing if I didn't come to her funeral,
she'd haunt me as a ghost.
She frightened me and I did go.
She returns anyway, taunting
my bookish ways. I know
nothing about sparrows—
if they prefer rye to cornbread,
make their nests in Florida
or hatch at the Bronx zoo.
In spring, the sparrows sputter
at Grandma's window. I offer
a muffin; they show no hunger.
I whistle; they fly away. Come back,
I call, seeing a language go extinct.

Nothing Important

Days of mist complete the season.
I move the clock ahead one hour
and find myself in a state of grace
that knows no freeze.

All winter, nothing important has died.

Hours before the equinox,
not a leaf whispers. Even unruly
ravens are at peace. The world waits
for the axis to turn.

With spring comes responsibility,
an impulse to affirm, to seed
our little clump, to leave
something of us behind.

Hint of Spring

After the black solstice, light extends
one minute by dawn, one by night,
so my mother said in her darkest days.

Haze shadows the grapestake fence,
hinting spring but sundown brings
chill, no rain. In drought, I carry

bath water in pots to the lemon tree.
Green fruit, bunched tight, clutches
my citric future. I need only enough

to squeeze lemons into tonic, add zest
to Moroccan salad. That crooked tree
is 75 years old, my role model. Sharing

pints and nozzles, whispers of love
we might last forever—
forever that is for two bent codgers.

Daylight Savings

Daylight! Daylight!
Out of control
the tempo speeds
whipping Time ahead—

As if new digits save
anything; as if savings collect
interest; as if Earth's
spin accelerates
or the sun stops for a drink
or the cow jumps over the moon.

What's early? Who's late?
Does the farmer win time
to milk that cow? Do bankers
get more hours to idle away?

I turn from God's time
to America's, ask forgiveness
for not waiting until dark,
for the pride of electricity,
for abandoning the stars.

Bait

Canvas backs cackle after sex
and smoothly swim apart. Trees
still bare, the woods don't filter
light. Green is greener, flesh
fleshier. Speechless deer stare
at the humping geese. We're all bait
for a passing creature. I hesitate
to approach strangers, afraid
to startle someone I may want to eat.

March Madness

She says the Sisters of Mercy
told her you can fall in a hole
but not fall in love. Maybe
they knew what they were talking about.
Maybe she does.
Every March I think of her.

She's from Minnesota, still below
zero in March, with long bronze hair,
a farm girl who calls me Zeke—
Ezekiel, after a Puritan zealot—and bats
her baby blue eyes, confesses
every March she has an affair.

If I knew Greek mythology,
I'd have precedents. Through
twenty-eight days of February
I count catastrophe coming. Every March
the same thing, sometimes
with the same person, sometimes
for a single day, sometimes forever.

Long ago she said, *Zeke*
this year will be different
this year will be you.
I was young. I replied
this year will be different
because it won't be me.

Her lips went white, cheeks red,
she swore a curse: *Zeke, I'll get you*
some day. Some day in March.
And since, I wondered how
and when. As days lengthen
and light lingers, I smell tragedy.

This year March struck
like the invisible hand of a god
or the devil. Poor Zeke. Just as
my hormones leaped toward spring
I lay bolted to a catheter,
beyond remorse, beyond desire.

Yes, my doctor says it's common
among aging men, remedied by
a slight procedure. I know better.
Years running away from fate comes
to this. How can anyone stop time?
Maybe next March will be different.

Lake Effect

Five winters in snow country, I marvel
at the strength of native-born neighbors,
storm windows hung in September, shovels
grating past May. When numbers drop
to 34 below, I say never again but a freak
blizzard catches me traveling, reveals
white beauty I missed, cascades spiraling
over the lake, ice sinking into stony clefts,
a dry nest set on a leafless tree.

Under full sun the next morning
a dozen ducks looking like toy boats
paddle in circles, a pond of melted snow.
Air brightens with birdsong. I hear
women raking in a garden, lifting
the odor of mulch. *It's not snowing,*
a man's voice shouts out the window.

Soon enough their thoughts will turn back
to splitting wood, insulation, rock salt.
Winter is serious: men fall
from icy roofs, skid into drifts. Reality
means furnace, flashlight, snow plough.
I watch two girls in red rubber boots stop
abruptly, bowing before a single daffodil.

PART 3

to study the light

The Murder of Crows

Under a gentle May sun, a spray
of moths rises like a fine geyser
shot from a crack in the sidewalk.

Life from the underworld winged
to fly but from a cloudless sky
a swarm of crows descends, filling
their yellow beaks with sweet
up-sent manna. At the crevice lip,
the quickest hunt and peck.

Shocked by violence, my voice breaks
the quiet. Hey, I shoo, stomp my feet.
The birds keep eating. More arrive.
Eat. Eat. Appetites alive, narcotic.
I witness nature's war—
bodies sighted, gulped, plundered.

Twenty minutes, the feast finished,
the pavement immaculate. Time's
been lived in a blink. Amid hungry
rage, birth, death, my heart speeds,
hears no moral, merely marvels.

The Longest Day

I wait a year for the day
light lasts longest, one minute
more than yesterday,
that minute everything

though today thick clouds refuse
to burn away. It's not
sunshine I crave
but clarity. Even without

the orange flash at sundown, I want
one minute more. Tomorrow
comes the tilt, blue globe tumbling
into the orbit of night.

The Fourth Falls on Friday

Quiet as Sunday morning, no mail,
newspapers thin, I awaken
as summer fog swims softly through
the willow leaves. If cloud-cover
holds, there'll be no fireworks tonight.

Nothing to distract cosmic melancholy—
glacial melting, the poor polar bears.
No techno-wizards to expunge
the drones (two wars, more to come).
No colored lights to erase midnight aches.

Still too early to predict, I heed
the nodding redwood,
needles firm, arms open
to the ocean's breeze, heavy air
hushing thoughts of leaving this bed.

Nowhere

I make no plan, nowhere
is where I want
to be, to vanish
in easy circles
outdoors on summer days.

Every duty's done
or damned.
I walk five miles
on Sawyer Trail,
no one can find me.

Above the reservoir, pale sky
and earth delineate, the lake
a perfect mirror. I go no
further than in-bound fog
hiding sundown.

Late when I return, I pass
my crowded desk, open
a Spanish wine. No time
to accomplish anything
that matters more.

Study the Light

Easy to spot the tourists—bare ankles,
> open toes, huddling in hooded sweatshirts.

Scant sunbathing, not much beach life
> but for blue-lipped children picking

shells, howling like maniacs
> as they run into the ocean and run out.

Summer comes in September. October starts
> the rainy season, lingering half the year.

Christmas likely to hit 70 or 40. Green-eyed geese
> bewildered, won't fly north *or* south.

The trick is to study the light,
> the year by dark, by bright.

Looking

The ocean is sneaky, low waves, rapid
surges, a drawn backward suck. Crab-like
a breaker leaps, catches a woman stepping
in foam, snatches the top of her swimsuit.
She screams, hands jump to her breasts.
Children nearby gawk at her panic, show
fear. An older boy moves closer. Her friend
rushes with a towel, his voice soothing.
The kids turn, scatter, but the youth
stays, entranced. Man and woman retreat
to a blanket. She dresses, gathers her bag
and basket. The boy struck rigid, his face
a mask. He's done nothing but
look, seen. Her image riveted, indelible,
for him, for me, forever.

Summer School

I'd spent one summer at the Post Office
hauling a 40-pound leather sack—
bills, letters, *Playboy* magazines
ogled before delivery. One patron
claimed she was Sigmund Freud's niece
and walked around in men's clothes.
One gent showed me nude photos
of Marilyn Monroe taken by his son.
And a doctor's wife once grabbed
the mail from my hands, turned
around and ordered me to zip up her dress
or zip it down, I forget which.
The next summer I ran a blouse shop,
accosted by foreign women asking
how centimeters translated
to inches. I measured their sizes
with bedroom eyes. Other women
attracted store detectives who
required my help chasing shoplifters.
One woman surrendered a radio
stowed inside her black brassiere.
When my friends boasted of sex
and how many women they knew,
I was not exactly uneducated,
having my share of stories to tell.

No Soap

I expect to idle near a river
barefoot, unwashed, all business
settled by neglect.

I call this a vacation, as in vacate.
Nothingness foams like laundry suds,
clears the brain of habits
that allow a person each morning
to put one arm into a clean sleeve,
then the other arm.

Anyway, what *is* clean?
How many showers are enough
if the neighbor arrives at midnight
wearing a see-through negligee
and her husband knocks just afterwards?

Goodbye troubles. Turn off the lights.
Hold the soap.

That Room

Usually there's a room,
pillows, blanket, a closet
not necessarily hangers.

The one I remember
has white tiles, sunlight simmering
off the sea. She hesitates
to draw the shades
while I study her olive-brown back.

Tongues taste of lemon
from the Bloody Marys, salt
from almonds. She knows
how to begin.

I follow directions. Between us
we get from somewhere
to everywhere, not always
by the easiest way.

That room at the edge of the Mediterranean
I don't expect to see again,
walls stained by droplets
maybe blood, paint peeling
over the bed, a chip of soap
that dissolves in a single wash,
the littlest things lasting forever.

One Word

Summer without heat, the sea sends
a gray drape inland, shadowing
the sun before night arrives. Under
a green canopy, I listen to the rhythmic
scrape of oak on pine, not
incidental to evening chill.

A hawk's perch atop the redwood
rocks like a ship in a gale. Venus
is blinking. The willows sigh,
yellow leaves fleeing into dry grass
as the fog shuffles closer,
stealing last light.

This modest spot I claim. If
someone came to share my world,
one word
would break the perfect peace.
I'd give it all to hear her voice.

The Wishing Tree 2: A Found Poem

On an olive tree in Port Costa, California near Suisun Bay, dozens of paper leaves tied by white string dangle from frail branches, their messages faded by weather and wind. In time, newcomers write different notes, reflecting timeless desire and temporal urge.

I wish to be successful and happy to fulfill my dreams & goals.

I wish that Marian and I remain good friends for a long time.

I wish for a long & happy life with my new beautiful wife.

I wish for rabbits and a phone.

For health peace and love for all same and different.

I wish my neighbor's cats would go away.

I wish to make my mommy proud.

I wish to grow two inches.

I wish for a successful business so I can provide for my family and not have to work at minimum wage any more.

I wish for a lifetime of cuddles, warm sweet kisses, and lots of laughs with the love of my life.

I wish I could think of a wish.

I wish to live without fear.

I wish I knew all that has been lost.

I wish what I'm about to do works.

I wish for my soul mate.

Heal quickly Paul.

I wish everyone can be awesome as me.

I wish for a touch.

I wish for rain to turn these hills green again.

I wish for Max to want to hug me in not a friend way.

I wish for prohibition of marijuana to end.

I wish for all the dogs in the world to be happy.

I wish to love myself as much as my cat loves my other cat.

Good man to come along.

I wish Manuela will recover completely from breast cancer.

I wish my parents would back off me a little.

I wish for a time machine so I could go back to Woodstock in 1969.

PART 4

before the real drama begins

A Glancing Blow

We meet by chance
the night of spring equinox,
a glancing blow. Something stirs
but in fact it's always stirring.

Yellow blossoms appear
on pear trees, azaleas bloom, I unzip
my jacket. Each year's the same
but this April I take notice.

I cut a sprig of lilacs from my yard,
a surprise for the one I give it to;
for me, too, surprise. Who am I,
this romantic stranger?

We thrive past summer solstice,
all July, find a ribbon
of green near the highway,
call it "Our Park."

We meet there at noon, after
work, late for everything else.
August it rains, we sit in my car,
sharing the last strawberries.

The sky darkens early, we wear
sweaters. Someone she knows sees
us together. Maples turning red
tell the story. We feel the chill.

Moonlit Fields

Late summer blues, I want
to recalibrate my calendar,
imagine the new year beginning
at spring equinox as the Puritans
measured time: not
by linear dates but as cycles
and seasons.

September happily migrates
to the first semester—before
the spectacle of football,
brass bands, stump orators—
before the real drama begins.
Autumn leaves, Thoreau says,
teach us how to die. But what
can a celibate know

of sensual nights
in moonlit harvest fields?
I visit the woodpile, select
kindling and willow, put on
the jazz, pour wine
into two glasses. And count
nine moons to the merry month.
Even stern Puritans knew May
delivers the most births.

Overnight Rain

First rain since winter subverts the seasons,
September is the new April. Overnight,
chartreuse blades crawl into the dry hills
like snakes entering a mirage. Finches—
a squadron streaks to the oaks pecking
at raindrops. Bay, pine, mysterious mulch
spice the air, arousing an adolescent deer.
The two-pronged youth refuses to yield,
dares me to open the gate. Black scat speaks
his graffiti. Drought's done its damage. Even
the drainpipe thumps like a heartbeat.
Everyone's edgy, circling puddles
before the next storm springs a leak.

The Truth Lies on Earth

The light is brighter
not because there is more
(there is less, forty minutes already)
but the angle shifts.

My eyelids pinch, overflowing
tears. A child on her way
to church asks, *Mister,*
why are you crying?

I point to the flaring sun
but the truth lies
on Earth, of course, the way
a person looks at darkness.

I come closer to my birth season.
Cherries have all been eaten,
tawny browns and reds bleed
through the curling leaves.

I'm eager
the way a doomed man prepares
for the next turn of the wheel,
the way October brings me renewal.

Prey

From where I walk in autumn shade,
I follow a woman moving at a modest pace,
the boulevard wide, divided by
traffic islands on which trees quiver,
yellow-brown leaves spilling
as the wind picks up, her blue coat lit
by the falling sun, a stage light
on a solitary figure, her steps deliberate
as if she's appearing in a scene.

And she is the scene
for the two men she doesn't see, doesn't
know yet the action about to occur
behind her wind-blown coat
while late light begins to diminish.

The man wearing a hooded sweatshirt
twenty or thirty feet ahead of me
on the opposite side of the boulevard
focuses on her movement in and out
of shadow, keeps behind her line
of sight, their distance constant.

His eyes fix on her blue outline, the way
a shooter in Kentucky on opening day
would peer through a telescopic lens
the length of a well-oiled rifle's barrel.
I watch him watching his blue deer—

a peculiar image except
for the man's intensity, sense of purpose,
steady gait, as if he's impelled
by a cavernous hunger, that hollow
inside a body no meal can satisfy—

and the woman unaware
wending her way alone, perhaps
from a thwarted shopping trip—
her arms free of baggage and burden—
or from an afternoon cappuccino
with a friend, perhaps at the café where
the man observed her departure.

Behind them, sighting his sighting
I see how one animal stalks another, how
early darkness lends opportunity, how
one can scent danger and do nothing.

The Visit

Air heavy, sea-cloud dripping
on shadowed glass, night-quiet
blankets the body. I'm awakened

by bad dreams, X-ray pictures
of my rib cage, bones scarred
by scalpel. I listen to my heart beat.

A deep breath, the lung good,
nothing there will happen soon.
All systems silent, ready to go.

Still, I rise in despair for the visit
to a brother who knows what
we all fear has settled inside.

He too counts pulses, breaths,
nights, the sunrise. No going back.
No forward ahead.

He knows his courage will not be
his reward but mine. He is showing
me how it can be done. *Like this.*

I take another breath, feel
the healed tissue clenching
in my chest. I dress in flannel

to enter the damp outside, will
myself forward, pass the willow tree,
steady on my way. *Like this.*

The Storm

The first gust of winter beats against
my door, shaking hinges. Time to trim
candles, unfold blankets before the wind
knocks out the power, freezes the furnace.

I'm all right but my brother needs help.
I pack snacks, batteries, a Dylan album
he loves but find he doesn't want music.
Startled from sleep, he asks who let me in.

I check if he's eaten, taken his pills, hoping
he'll answer my unasked question. He won't.
I stay, hearing his hard breath, body twitching
while the brute outdoors gets ready to strike.

PART 5

no matter how lonely

The Soul of Home

She enters my dream
as dawn passes the shade,
her voice silky.

Thirty five years.

Much younger, black waves,
shoulders bare, a print dress.
She crosses the threshold,
whispers again

Time to come home.

My mother, near 90,
as if calling from downstairs
summons me from sleep.

Isn't it time?

The words her prayer,
the dream mine:
What am I waiting for?

Motherless Child

Teary green eyes,
my mother humming the tune
to the little girl she lost,

curly black hair, thin lips,
ruby ring around her neck.

A long way from home

Who never came home,
naked on white. Never
sang, never sung to.

I feel like I'm almost gone

Velvet, my mother's voice
telling me, this child,
if my sister lived
no need for me.

Like a motherless child
Way up in that heavenly land

For this child
no need to wonder
no need
to sing in her place.

So far, so far, so far
Mama from you

For My Sister Patricia

Two sisters before me,
one still-born
whose name, if
it belongs to someone
alive, I always forget.

Whenever I struggle to remember
a woman's name
my lost sister
enters the room.

Nothing else marks her memory
except what my other sister
thinks and she never says.

No one even knows
she was.

What She Looks Like

My mother drives on Northern Boulevard,
white hair billowing like Einstein's aura.
Her license celebrates its diamond anniversary.

She says, *when your father sees me,*
he'll be surprised what I look like.
She's collecting facts for him, headlines

and hemlines, pop tunes. She plans
to entertain Daddy with everything he missed
when they meet, trip the light fantastic.

The Music Teacher

Half my life my father's dead.
Now his students, my classmates
summon a reunion, fifty years
since graduation, come looking
for the music teacher, find me
no longer the boy with a horn.

I tell how he became
The Old Timer—from tinkering
with fiddles, flutes, clarinets,
he adopted decrepit antiques—
wooden works, wags on the wall—
taught old clocks to whistle
quarters and hours, but irregularly
so each could solo its tune.

I tell about his gospel,
not once a prayer
unless we count *Goddam*—
but Sunday mornings near the end
he strolled around the corner
to the white clapboard house
revived as an evangelical church
to piano play the hymnal blues
(the only witness who was white)
just for the hell of singing out
Hallelujah! Roll, Jordan, Roll.

I tell them more than I need to
but I'm wrapped in the gifts
a man bequeaths his son, least
the subject he taught everyone else.
My Dad knew the worth of time.

A Child's Mistake

Sometimes I lose the sound
of my father's voice, time's whirlpool
drenching the volume. On the last
Mother's Day of his life, he made
audio tape of scratchy vinyl—
Robeson's *Old Man River,*
Marian Anderson's *Motherless Child*—
his conversation interspersing tunes
from my childhood. I cannot bear
to play it. Instead I concentrate
on my first bedroom, overhearing
piano lessons he gave at home.
I learned every note of Chopin
by heart, listening to hapless pupils
struggle with the keys. It comes back,
this most lucid moment, a child's mistake
prompting my father's baritone
to ring through the rooms,
E-flat. E-flat—perfect pitch
mending the tear in my memory.

The Radio between Us

I steered my father's Buick toward the sun,
our roles reversed, the radio between us.
We loved a soloist's virtuosity.

He chose long-hair classics, favored form,
punctuation. I had no patience, he said;
did inspiration exceed implementation?

I spoke for impulse, riffs—when red lights
flashing interrupted, an ambulance
startling us into silence—

slowly a tune on the radio: fast-fingering
alto sax, trumpeter inserting a flare of brass.
Miles Davis, we said together just as the siren

woofed, shook us into happy counterpoint.
We didn't speak again, those last moments
we had alone, just listened, *Kind of Blue.*

The Old Timer

My father's clocks tick and wag
as he left them the last night,
reaching for one of his beauties.
They died together in tight embrace,
mapping a gash in the plaster wall.

Time didn't stop for my mother.
She sold off that Temptress, but
kept pulling the weights, turning
brass keys, kept his hours tuned
until the day they'd meet.

Now everything's gone haywire:
the whistling Yankee Peddler lost
his hand, the Cuckoo never caws,
oaken Grandfather slipped a disk.
Mother worries if he'll be angry.

Bessie Alone

Years ripple like waves
of white lace against her shore.
The gold watch swivels
on her shriveling wrist,
the red sweater swims
as her body relinquishes.

She fidgets on a flowered couch,
tests the soil in her potted plants,
ignores the woman
who will drive her to the clinic.

She refuses to speak about what's known.
Years of waiting, the end has come
abruptly.

Months since she's been outside
this late, my mother beelines
to the pier's edge, thrilled
to watch gulls hovering,
a trawler land its catch.

Across the bay a cherry willow
droops in bloom, purples
the last light. Her eyes follow
a wedge of geese winging home.
Her lips open, she lacks for words.

She knows at 96 and doesn't want
to know, plans to recover, slide
her slim body behind the wheel,
take herself to market.
She will not discuss the issues—
transition, assistance. She dismisses

the caretaker from Jamaica,
pleasant but a poor cleaner.
I explain her choices do not
include a plunge off the bridge.

She begins to bargain,
fishing for escape, annoyed
by sweet talk. She knows what
comes next, how little I know.

Round-faced, smiling Maureen escorts
my mother to the bingo-entertainment center,
shows off a blank four-foot ice-blue screen.
As if tossing stardust to an old prospector,
she opens an alcove stocked with decaf and tea,
a wall-length freezer, says ice cream is free.

Upstairs, she unveils a widow's paradise:
dresser, end table, half a fridge, half a twin bed,
a microwave—wink—to soften the ice cream.

No, says my hard of hearing mother too loudly,
the ice cream is not free. I'll be paying for it
and the bingo too—though I wouldn't go near
either one, no matter how lonely I feel.

I can't expect a 96-year old
to change her personality.
When I look at her conditions:
frailty, fear of strangers living
in her house, repulsion
at the sanitized residence
she visited yesterday, I ask
what can I learn, knowing
nothing good can come
from somebody's loss.

The check book's unbalanced,
auto insurance cancelled (non-payment),
taxes in default. She remembers
handling the household,
each and every penny.
Now the barley soup is cold,
milk's sour, she's run out of tea.
The senile ones only bother
other people, she explains,
I depress myself.

Not the confusions of an old woman
calling her daughter by another's name.
Not conflated memories of her honeymoon
with a trip she took after her husband died—
merely leakage of a rusty bucket,
buttons fallen off a comfortable coat.

My mother knows the details, first
address to last, top floor apartment
467 East 169TH Street, the Bronx, gas lights
going electric, novelty of the phone,
questions on high school chemistry tests—

but no one's around to share longevity's
wonder, snippets alive in a solitary brain.

When she is 98, my mother recites
every address she's ever had, explaining
her mother chose the top floor
in walk-up buildings not because
they were cheap but she didn't want
to hear footsteps over her head.

My mother in the same breath says
don't plant grass on my grave. Put in
azalea. I'll be dead a long time.

※

She liked those days, me sitting
in my father's rocking chair,
she on the couch, legs crossed,
wool in her lap, needles clicking.

I give her prompts, ask about cousins,
one who adopted a daughter
illegally, one with a nervous breakdown.

She hesitates, looks out the window, begins
her yarn always in 1933 when she met
my Dad, laughing at the prices—
five pounds of peaches for a dime,
how he ate every one in a night, admitting
later, *No wonder I'm not hungry.*

I've heard her scripts, tunes
unchanging, always with a moral.
To her, everything is fated
at birth, her problems, her health,
even her pride, living alone.

※

My mother's morning song
an unfamiliar squawk, croaks
warning. Something's wrong,
startles her: how devious age
attacks, knife at the throat,
this zealous cancer, good skin
bristles into gooseflesh.

※

I offer comfort
when there is no comfort,
her breath constrained.
She hoped for something fast,
lucid. The pliant tube,
stiff as a straw, flutes
accompaniments
to words she barely hears.
Never the right time, she says,
disbelieves her ears.

At 98 nothing specific ails her
though she has no chance
of feeling better. OK, she says,
provided it doesn't get worse.

She's sung that song for decades,
her widowhood stretching
longer than marriage, blames
father's death for her emptiness.

The void's contagious—no end
to the interminable. I'm older now
than she was when. When his train
left the station, when waiting began.

I concentrate on the clack
of a tray, faucet drizzles,
whatever she experiences
of the outside world inside
her room, until I reach through
near deafness to awaken her.
A watery breath passes for talk.
I say thanks and love, softly
not to startle her, just to be
here, permit her release.

✹

After Mama died, we had to sell the house
she'd lived in for half her century
and the estate, so-called, hundreds
of plastic cups and dress hangers,
envelopes of granulated sugar, puzzles,
what a woman keeps for a rainy day.

Spatters, cobwebs wiped from walls,
closets cleared of pocketbooks, gift boxes
with tags attached, a mirror cloudy
as her hearing. I give posthumously
the help she refused—rub away a smudge
her hand pressed whenever she passed.

Her world shrinking, she simplified, saying
No to cell phone, microwave, visitors—
but tended the African violets as children.
Dry leaves linger where her finger pressed
soil. I bring in water from the tap still
dripping at the faucet she forbade me to fix.

Winter Sleep

She died at winter solstice,
hours before the 75TH year
of her marriage. My mother counted
the calendar, knew the next day
would lighten by one minute.

She had a witch's knack, could
predict with perfection
the sex of unborn children, spoke
answers before questions, cracked
puzzles like a maven.

She told vivid tales, capturing
the excitement of electricity—
What was that? she'd shriek
with delight—remembering
the magic of incandescent bulbs,

but she preferred the shadows,
to blanket her body
in the wool of solitude, refusing
to brighten the gloom of December.

In darkness, she recited lyrics
to dispel the slow hours, wanted
no bedside lamp
to outshine her memory.

Before sunrise on the darkest day,
she chose her hour,
departed into the pit of night.

ACKNOWLEDGMENTS

The Aurorean:	"Before Sunrise"; "Amherst" (nominated for Pushcart Prize)
Catamaran Literary Review:	"Destiny"
Cultural Weekly:	"Bait"; "Looking"; "Turning"
Heavy Bear:	"The Radio between Us"
Jewish Currents:	"Daylight Savings"; "Nothing Important"
Marin Poetry Center Anthology 2016:	"In the Fourth Year of Drought"
Poecology:	"Sparrows"
Sand Hill Review:	"The Music Teacher"
Spillway:	"Overnight Rain"
Willow Glen Poetry:	"March Madness"

Thanks

My Saturday Morning poets continue to inspire and nourish me: Terry
Adams, Anne Chelek, Casey FitzSimons, Esther Kamkar, Muriel Karr, Harry
Lafnear, and Lee Rossi know how to keep a poet honest. Charlotte Muse and
Richard Silberg generously shared their opinions of the emerging manuscript.
John Daniel and Jane Spiro as ever bring critical delight. I also thank my hosts
at various readings for the opportunity to test my voice aloud: Joyce Jenkins of
Poetry Flash; Christine & Dennis Richardson of Willow Glen; Peter Stansky
whose Company of Authors at Stanford is always a treat; Andrew Lee at the
Puffin Foundation series in Teaneck, New Jersey; Gary Jones at the American
International College in Springfield, Massachusetts; Ramon & Judy Sender of
San Francisco's Odd Monday Series; Sandra Anfang of the Rivertown poets in
Petaluma; Sherri Rose-Walker of the Florey's series in Pacifica; Erica Goss
Poet Laureate Emerita of the Poetry Kitchen; Connie Post at the Valona series
in Crockett that led to "The Wishing Tree 2," as well as the usual suspects at
Not Yet Dead Poets and Waverley Writers. Much delight, too, for this book's
appearance goes to Debra Turner of dtDesign. Turning Point's Kevin Walzer
and Lori Jareo have once again been a pleasure to work with. Who matters most
to me in poetry (and everything else) is Jeannette Ferrary. Thanks!

About the Author

The Truth Lies on Earth, Peter Neil Carroll's fourth volume of poetry, unravels the skeins between time and place, tracking seasonal change and passage of generations. His previous collections include *Fracking Dakota: Poems for a Wounded Land* (Turning Point, 2015) and *A Child Turns Back to Wave: Poetry of Lost Places* (2012), which won the Prize Americana from the Institute for the Study of American Popular Culture. An earlier volume, *Riverborne: A Mississippi Requiem* (2008), explores the lonely world of America's great river. His poems have appeared in *The Aurorean, Catamaran Literary Review, Cultural Weekly, Sand Hill Review, Southern Humanities Review, Spillway, Tar River Poetry Review,* and *Verse Daily.* He has published over twenty books, including the memoir, *Keeping Time* (2011). He has taught creative writing at the University of San Francisco, taught history and American Studies at Stanford and Berkeley, hosted "Booktalk" on Pacifica Radio, and edited the *San Francisco Review of Books.* He is currently Poetry Moderator of Portside.org and lives in northern California with the writer/photographer Jeannette Ferrary.

Praise for *The Truth Lies on Earth*

"No one explores the circularity of life, its rhythms, pitfalls, and small miracles, better than Peter Neil Carroll, a master at weaving nature into narrative. What I like best in this fine collection are the poems about women. Carroll's love of strong, self-sufficient women —'what she required she'd find/in herself'— celebrates both women he knew and those he could only fantasize about. Fierce, reflective and reverent, his poetry is filled with wisdom and wry wit. 'The trick,' Carroll tells us, 'is to study the light/the year by dark, by bright.' No one says it better."—Alexis Rhone Fancher, Poetry Editor, *Cultural Weekly*

"*The Truth Lies on Earth* is a place of both quietude and raucous celebration. Find here the gorgeous cyclical world we share with the cormorant and willow and every creature in between, rendered without flinching and infused with the difficult process of letting go."—Caroline Goodwin, First San Mateo County Poet Laureate, author of *Peregrine* and *Trapline*

"In his latest book, Peter Neil Carroll explores the changing natural and human landscape with an observant eye. In poems that are meditative, sometimes lonely, Carroll is the eavesdropper in a café, the unseen observer on a beach, a student of light, of seasons, of days that grow and diminish by the minute. Rarely judgmental, the poems show us 'rage, birth, death,' with a heart that 'hears no moral, merely marvels.' The book culminates in a long, wonderful elegy for his mother that is simply terrific."— Roy Mash, author of *Buyer's Remorse*

Also by Peter Neil Carroll

Fracking Dakota: Poems for a Wounded Land (2015)
A Child Turns Back to Wave: Poetry of Lost Places (2012)
Riverborne: A Mississippi Requiem (2008)

A Note on the Type

Designed by Zuzana Licko in 1996, Mrs Eaves is a variant of the classic Baskerville font that originated in England in the 1750s. This highly readable font is primarily used in book design.

છ   છ   છ   છ   છ   છ

Made in the USA
Lexington, KY
11 February 2017